CIVIL DISOBEDIENCE:
AID OR HINDRANCE TO JUSTICE?

*Second in the sixth series of Rational Debates
sponsored by the American Enterprise Institute
held at
American Enterprise Institute
Washington, D.C.*

ROBERT GORALSKI
Moderator

CIVIL DISOBEDIENCE:
AID OR HINDRANCE TO JUSTICE?

William Sloane Coffin, Jr.
Morris I. Leibman

RATIONAL DEBATE SERIES

American Enterprise Institute for Public Policy Research
Washington, D.C.

Library of Congress Catalog Card Number L.C. 72-88233

FOREWORD

"If a man does not keep pace with his companions, perhaps it is because he hears a different drummer." So wrote Henry David Thoreau. But how far out of step may a member of civil society justly go? Is the drummer of individual conscience sufficient authority for a person to disregard law which he believes to be immoral? Is one morally justified in breaking proper laws to protest injustice in another sphere? Even if the foregoing questions can be answered "yes," does such conduct advance the cause of justice, or does it undermine it by condoning lawlessness?

Were America a totalitarian state, the answers to such questions would, for most, be obvious. But America is not totalitarian; we have a system of law which is intended to permit peaceful change. Some Americans think it works, some do not. Many of the latter are today engaging in acts of civil disobedience, and there rages a great debate over the efficacy of such action as a means for advancing justice.

This debate, featuring two thoughtful men who agree there is injustice in the United States but who strongly disagree about how to end it, is a worthy contribution to reasoned consideration of this important issue. The Reverend William Sloane Coffin, Jr. advocates civil disobedience in the service of what he considers a higher justice than that embodied in the *positive law*. Morris Leibman champions the cause of working through the "system."

Neither man may persuade the reader of his view, but there is no doubt that this lively exchange will set one thinking. Since it is our purpose at the American Enterprise Institute to promote serious reflection on major public policy issues, we are pleased to add this volume to our sixth annual series of Rational Debates.

August 1972

William J. Baroody
President
American Enterprise Institute
for Public Policy Research

CONTENTS

FIRST LECTURE

WILLIAM SLOANE COFFIN, JR.

At times civil disobedience has certainly been a hindrance to justice; too often the wrong people do the wrong thing at the wrong time. At other times, however, civil disobedience has greatly aided justice.

This contention becomes clear when one considers how many of those we today regard as heroes were notorious law breakers in their time. To cite a few Biblical examples: Moses was a wanted man, and David an outlaw; Isaiah and Jeremiah were both accused of conspiracy and treason (which is perhaps why we read in Isaiah "Thus saith the Lord: 'Do not call conspiracy all that this people call conspiracy'"). Shadrach, Meshach, and Abednego are known and known only for their "divine disobedience." Jesus transgressed both the civil and the religious law, claiming that "the Sabbath belongs to man, not man to the Sabbath," and of course was executed as a traitor. His disciples broke laws with such regularity that someone recently suggested that the "Acts of the Apostles" could be retitled the "Arrests of the Apostles." And the Jewish and Roman laws they broke were by the standards of the time far from cruel.

All these people—not to mention Socrates, Thoreau, Gandhi, and King—all these people are heroes to us today because they represent those individual consciences of the world which, as opposed to the mass mind, best represent the universal conscience of mankind.

1

Civil disobedience has effectively been practiced by groups as well, as a quick reading of American history will show. Seventeenth century Quakers broke many laws in Virginia and in Massachusetts. In the eighteenth century the followers of Washington, Franklin, Hamilton, Jefferson, and Adams were traitors all, until success crowned their efforts and they became great patriots! In the nineteenth century the abolitionists defied the Fugitive Slave Act. In the first half of the twentieth century the suffragettes engaged in illegal demonstrations, as did the labor movement with its strikes, boycotts and sit-ins, all of which were illegal at the time. Finally, in the second half of our century dozens of segregationist laws were broken by thousands of members of the so-called civil rights movement.

Why did these individuals and groups engage in civil disobedience? Because, to paraphrase Jesus, the law belongs to man, not man to the law. Put differently, the law never represents pure justice, but only about as much justice as any given people at any given time will sanction. The law, in other words, does not so much instruct as reflect public opinion. Therefore, if the law is to reflect more, and reject less, man's highest notions of justice, someone has constantly to provoke change—the change new laws will hopefully some day embody. The primary function of civil disobedience, then, is to provoke this change.

Civil disobedience often becomes necessary where change is most difficult to provoke, namely where people's personal interests are most directly affected. In such areas people tend to be motivated not by love of truth but by fear of truth, a fear that prompts them to retreat into a callous and unenlightened selfishness.

Too often we forget that majority rule can never be equated with the rule of conscience. After all, the majority of our citizens have in the past supported slavery and child labor, and today still support various forms of racial discrimination, sex discrimination, slums, and a penal system far more punitive than curative.

Furthermore, just as powerful nations dominate the international community, so powerful individuals or groups can dominate a domestic community, be it a small town, a big city, or a nation. The powerful have many legal forms of coercion—economic power, access to government, propaganda. So it is hardly surprising to see the law protecting the rich and powerful more often than it helps the poor and the weak.

To see how law serves power we have only to look at the history of the labor movement in this country. I know of no mine or factory owner who was ever arrested for denying his miners or workers their right of free speech. But I know that hundreds of miners and workers in Washington, Colorado, Pennsylvania, and Massachusetts were imprisoned merely for exercising that constitutional right.

And what are we to say when four college students at Kent State are shot down in full public view, when an FBI investigation puts the responsibility on the national guard, and when the only ones accused of crimes are the victims' fellow students?

In response to all these considerations, it seems to me we have to say two things: the first is that the law, while worthy of respect, is not deserving of unreasoning obedience. If we are to serve our country with our consciences we must recognize that what is most important is not what the law requires but what justice demands. Thoreau once said, "We must be men first and subjects afterwards."

Secondly, we must recognize that justice is a higher social goal than law and order. I stress this proposition because it is so easy for justice to be sacrificed on the altars of stability. Those who "have it made" are always chary of those "on the make," and every dispute between them tends to emphasize the means over the ends. Rarely do the powerful ask which side is struggling for greater justice; rarely do the powerful see what is clear to me, that a conflict for the emancipation of a race or a class or a nation has more moral justification than a law to perpetuate privileges. In other words, the oppressed have a higher moral right to challenge oppression than oppressors have to maintain it.

Turning now to civil disobedience as a means, let us recognize that it has traditionally taken two forms. The first seeks only to test the legality of a law. Martin Luther King believed that, on his side, were both his conscience and the United States Constitution. And time and again he was proved right as the Supreme Court decided that it was not King but the segregationists he opposed who were civilly disobedient. The municipal and state laws they had implemented proved unconstitutional when tested.

A second type of disobedience recognizes the legality of the law, but feels its inhumanity to be so great as to make obedience to it morally impossible. Much opposition to military conscription has traditionally fallen into this category,

4

particularly when a country is engaged in a war as unpopular as the war in Vietnam.

The second kind of disobedience preserves an individual's moral self-respect. But it can also be politically effective, especially when those who engage in it are nonviolent, do not infringe on the civil liberties of others, and accept the legal consequences of their actions. I have in mind, for example, those who, in response to the Vietnam war, refused induction and went to jail.

When property is damaged, the political effectiveness becomes more problematical. The Catonsville Nine, for example, were not immediately effective. However, it was not long before the gentle spirit of those involved and the talented writing of Father Daniel Berrigan began to reach and convert many hearts. Actually, most acts of civil disobedience tend to become more influential with the passage of time. Thoreau is an obvious case in point—and, to return to the Catonsville group, there is no doubt that thirty years from now the Berrigan brothers will be genuine folk heroes, widely celebrated in song and story and celluloid.

When violence to persons is involved, the effectiveness of civil disobedience becomes *truly* problematical, if only because public attention tends to center on the violence itself. But if one's heart can go out to St. Peter cutting off the ear of the High Priest's servant in the Garden of Gethsemane, one's heart should be able to go out to all who are moved to violence because of the sufferings of others. Violence can be an expression of charity, albeit a distortion of it. Indifference, on the other hand, can only be the perfection of egoism. So it remains an open question as to whether it is worse to have blood on one's hands or water like Pilate.

My own view is that indifference is finally the greatest promoter of violence. President Kennedy was right when he said that those who make peaceful evolution impossible make violent revolution inevitable.

As regards violent revolution, almost all Americans revere their own as an aid to justice, and probably most feel the same way about the American Civil War. However, most Americans take a dimmer view of the Russian and the Chinese revolutions, and of course when Blacks in America rise up to fight for equal rights, the descendants of Thomas Jefferson tend to make like George the Third! This thought leads me to mention—but time allows no elaboration—the kind of disobedience that in my view most hinders the progress of justice. I have in mind unconstitutional acts undertaken by the United States government itself.

I said the law tends to reflect rather than to instruct public opinion. There are times, however, when the reverse should be true, times when the law needs to temper passion and to direct political leaders tempted to do what is politic at the expense of what is right. In recent years our leaders have badly betrayed the requirements of the United States Constitution. For example, it is hard to argue for the constitutionality of the original involvement of the United States in Vietnam, for the lies revealed in the Pentagon Papers, for the inhumane prosecution of the war in clear violation of rules of war officially ratified by the United States government, and for the extensive bombing undertaken by the Nixon administration despite the wishes of the Congress clearly expressed in Title 6 of the Military Procurement Act of 1972.

As regards domestic affairs, the Nixon administration has repeatedly failed to implement—and despite campaign promises to the contrary—the requirements of both the Fourteenth and the Fifteenth Amendments. Further, no loyal American can be happy with this statement of Lawrence Baskin, staff director and chief counsel of the Senate Subcommittee on Constitutional Rights: "The only part of the Bill of Rights that the [Nixon] Administration hasn't either rewritten or violated is the only one it should have—the right to bear arms."

It is the failure of the government to implement constitutional requirements that in my judgment constitutes today the greatest menace to democracy as we know it.

SECOND LECTURE

MORRIS I. LEIBMAN

Turning and turning in the widening gyre
The falcon cannot hear the falconer;
Things fall apart; the centre cannot hold;
Mere anarchy is loosed upon the world,
The blood-dimmed tide is loosed, and everywhere
The ceremony of innocence is drowned;
The best lack all conviction, while the worst
Are full of passionate intensity.

William Butler Yeats

I am for law and order.

I oppose civil disobedience.

The simplicity of these statements lies only on the surface.

We must, like Whitehead, "Seek simplicity but distrust it," particularly now that fads and fashion grip the country, even in the field of ideas.

The serious and precise exploration of ideas is particularly difficult in a time which welcomes stereotypes, slogans and simple solutions, and in which headlines are accepted as adequate summaries of complex issues. When man's historic problems are, far too often, approached with catch phrases, one would at least expect some evidence of vestigial guilt on the part of those proposing the easy remedies. But if there is such guilt, it is rejected with self-righteous cries of morality, conscience, love and peace—with no attempt to define the words used. Television, with its limitations and attention-getting emphasis, well serves this popular superficiality.

Under such conditions, demagoguery and fanaticism flourish. An intellectual muddle is generated and such concepts as "code words" are in vogue. Law and order have been fiercely attacked in this climate as nothing more than "code words" for repression and fascism. I must, therefore, begin with an explanation and a definition. When I say I am for "law and order" I mean American law and order, which to me means the just enforcement of our laws under our system of justice—not Torquemada's. Law and justice result in order, as I use the word, because our legal and constitutional system, with its Bill of Rights and set procedures, recognizes that justice and liberty are man's finest bridge to the achievement of human dignity and brotherhood. It is precisely because I believe in man's humanity rather than his inhumanity that I reject civil disobedience.

In current parlance the term "civil disobedience" is supposed to describe a morally justifiable violation of the law. The phrase is presumably designed to distinguish certain conduct from ordinary disobedience and from crime. Like most slogans devised or resurrected for their propaganda value, the phrase obscures rather than promotes analysis. In particular the adjective "civil" is both misleading and contradictory.

In democratic societies any violation of the law is an uncivil act. This is true notwithstanding the motives of the violators. The violation is an assault on civil and social cohesion, the very basis of the peaceful interaction of men as "political animals." Such an act is always disruptive and to describe it as "civil" is a contradiction in terms. Our society is a society created within the rule of law. As Father John Courtney Murray has said of civil society:

> It is in direct contrast with the passionate fanaticism of the Jacobin: "Be my brother or I'll kill you!" Ideally, I suppose, there should be only one passion in the city— the passion for justice. But the will to justice, though it engages the heart, finds its measure as it finds its origin in intelligence, in a clear understanding of what is due to the equal citizen from the City and to the City from the citizenry according to the mode of their equality. This commonly shared will to justice is the ground of civil amity as it is also the ground of that unity which is called peace. This unity, qualified by amity, is the highest good of the civil multitude and the perfection of its civility.[1]

Thus, individual or group violation of the law is the very antithesis of civil conduct.

It would be more accurate, I suggest, if the proponents of such violations were to use the term "justifiable disobedience," which at least has the merit of accurately describing their claims. They admit the disobedience, but claim that their acts are justifiable. Increasingly, the disobedients do not even bother to pretend that their behavior is "civil," either in the sense of supporting our civil society or as a civilized way of dealing with other human beings. Indeed, they often flaunt their incivility. It is my contention that, just as the term "civil disobedience" is semantically inaccurate, so the concept

13

of "justifiable disobedience" is morally untenable. Justifiable disobedience is allegedly

1. morally motivated,
2. performed openly and publicly,
3. accompanied by a willingness to accept the punishment, and
4. harmless to others.

Although these characterizations provide a superficial veneer of philosophic respectability, they do not withstand analysis. In the first place, there is simply no objective test for establishing either sincerity or morality of motive. Men do not lightly admit to evil motives, even to themselves. The example of modern tyrants demonstrates that mere dedication to a cause is no guarantee of moral value or righteous judgment. But those who plead morality as a reason for breaking the law also set themselves up as judges—and the only judges —of their own actions. In short, the question of moral justification is always disputable, never resolvable, and subject to the worst weaknesses of human passion. It provides no test for deciding when it might be acceptable to violate the law. Far less does it provide a yardstick for determining which laws ought to be violated.

Second, the publicity given to a violation is equally irrelevant, since public illegality sets an example which is certain to be abused. The courts have pointed out that openness excuses neither a crime nor a conspiracy. If anything, open violations do more damage to society than covert ones.

Third, the willingness to accept the punishment is no justification for the violation of the law. In theory, every one breaking a law invites punishment. One should not be murdered simply because a killer is willing to suffer imprisonment or even death. At most, the willingness to accept punishment is an inadequate notion absurdly applied to determine the moral nobility of a particular violator. George F. Kennan points out:

> The violation of the law is not, in the moral and philosophic sense, a privilege that lies offered for sale with a given price tag like an object in a supermarket, available to anyone who has the price and is willing to pay for it. It is not like the privilege of breaking çrockery in a tent at the country fair for a quarter a shot. Respect for the law is not an obligation which is exhausted or obliterated by willingness to accept the penalty for breaking it.
>
> To hold otherwise would be to place the privilege of lawbreaking preferentially in the hands of the affluent, to make respect for law a commercial proposition rather than a civic duty and to deny any authority of law independent of the sanctions established against its violation. It would then be all right for a man to create false fire alarms or frivolously to pull the emergency cord on the train, or to do any number of other things that endangered or inconvenienced other people, provided only he was prepared to accept the penalties of so doing. Surely, lawlessness and civil disobedience cannot be condoned or tolerated on this ground; and those of us who care for the good order of society have no choice but to resist attempts at its violation, when this is their only justification.[2]

Furthermore despite the claim of willingness to accept punishment, the disobedients have been extremely reluctant to do so, and have used mass disobedience and demands for amnesty to avoid it.

At this point it should be made clear that the so-called "test case" is not civil disobedience. A test case occurs because an individual has *reason* to believe that a statute does not have the force of law because it is unconstitutional. If the individual's belief is wrong then he must pay the penalty whether he wants to or not. Only one case by one individual of a minimal degree of violation is needed to test a law's constitutionality and hence, validity. The test case procedure is a recognized and necessary method of questioning whether a law is within our constitutional system. It is based on reason, as well as on the federal and various state constitutions, and not on "higher laws" per se. It is an objective process not based on conscience or moral belief.

Finally, the argument that such violations cause no harm to others is untenable. Illegal public acts do both immediate and long-term harm to society. The cases of harm done to specific individuals by recent acts of disobedience are too numerous to recount in the space and time provided. Secondary harm has also been done to an even vaster number of specific individuals in the forms of higher costs, lost opportunities, and various restrictions on individual freedoms. Judge Learned Hand once remarked that "When Plato tried to define justice he found that he could not stop short of building a commonwealth. No concept would answer which did not comprise the sum of the citizens' relations to the state at large."[3] Violations of the law constitute a direct attack on those relations, and therefore undermine the building of a

16

just society. Because this fact is so often ignored, it is useful to consider briefly the existing relationships in our society.

In considering the nature of our society under the rule of law, I start with certain general assumptions about our political structure:

1. In the complex world of man, the claims of justice constantly collide. The resolution of such collisions has to occur through a procedural system rather than through the unfettered exercise of the individual will. The uniqueness of America—its miracle—lies in its processes and procedures for implementing justice. These processes and procedures reflect an understanding of human nature grounded in experience; they are the result of the lessons of hundreds of years of failures to achieve a just system.

2. A just *system* is essential because no single human law can ever be perfectly "just." Therefore, the just *system* includes multiple opportunities for peaceful change and development. In few other societies are thousands of men daily engaged in courts, councils, legislatures and agencies, constantly amending and changing the law. Every law is subject to this process. It is a perpetual process of improvement.

3. Under these circumstances it is grossly presumptuous for one man to attempt to justify the violation of a law simply because he, himself, deems that law to be unjust. No law exists which does not cause suffering to someone, even in such mundane areas as traffic, taxing and zoning. If we assume that no law can bring about perfect justice, then we must be particularly dedicated to a *system* of

17

justice which seeks, even if it can never obtain, perfect justice.

With these principles in mind we can proceed to consider certain basic features of our political system.

American society is fundamentally democratic. By this I mean that the vast majority of its adult citizens are able to influence the law by freely voting for their own representatives. In fact, the number of people who have the right to vote has been significantly expanded in recent years. There have been no societies in world history where so many have had access to the political process. We have become so accustomed to this principle that we tend to forget how rare it really is. Democratic societies are a tiny minority of those known to history. Most men now living do not enjoy these rights, and this fact alone should make us cherish our political system even though it is not perfect. American democracy offers an almost unique system of constitutional democratic institutions. The system incorporates representative government, the separation of powers, the Bill of Rights, judicial review and due process. In addition there are the separations and interplay of local, state, and federal relationships. There are opportunities in the governing process for a free press, political organizations, public interest groups, independent organizations, and private social welfare agencies of every description. On top of all this a vast area of freedom is allowed to individuals to cooperate through business, labor, schools and foundations.

American society is fundamentally egalitarian. By this I simply mean that our laws make no basic distinction between citizens. In this area we have made great strides in recent years toward the ideal, and our progress is clear, whether viewed historically or as compared with the world at large.

American society is basically rational and humane. By this I mean that it usually practices the virtues of tolerance, humility and resort to reason.

No human institution can be perfect. The justice of a system must be judged by standards which are comparative rather than utopian. A convenient set of humane measurements is provided by the United Nations Declaration of Human Rights. These rights are enumerated as the rights to: life; liberty; security of person; freedom from slavery; freedom from torture; equality before the law and the equal protection of the law; access to judicial tribunals; protection from arbitrary arrest, detention or exile; fair and public trials; the presumption of innocence; notice of the illegality of an action; privacy; freedom of movement and residence; national citizenship; freedom to marry and create a family; ownership of property; freedom of thought, conscience and religion; freedom of opinion and expression; freedom of peaceful assembly and association; representative government; equal access to public service; genuine free elections with universal and equal suffrage; social security; freedom of employment; equal pay for equal work; to form and join trade unions; rest and leisure; an adequate standard of living; free education; to participate in the cultural life of the community; and it is further stated in the declaration:

Article 28. Everyone is entitled to a social and international order in which the rights and freedoms set forth in this declaration can be fully realized.

Article 29(1) Everyone has duties to the community in which alone the free and full development of his personality is possible.

(2) In the exercise of his rights and freedoms, everyone shall be subject only to such limitations as are determined by law solely for the purpose of securing due recognition and respect for the rights and freedoms of others and of meeting the just requirements of morality, public order and the general welfare in a democratic society.

While in any area designated by this declaration we have need for improvement, there is no reason for Americans to be ashamed. These ends are more closely approximated in America today than in any other nation at this or any other time in world history.

Even if we assume that civil disobedience is all that its most idealistic proponents claim it to be, it is inconsistent with the most admirable qualities of American society and is profoundly antidemocratic. The violation of a law duly enacted by a majority can never be anything else. There should be absolutely no mistake about this point. On it hangs a critical failing of the entire theory of civil disobedience.

This antidemocratic bias has in fact been openly conceded by the advocates of violation. Thoreau makes his full political philosophy very clear at the beginning of "On the Duty of Civil Disobedience." He is an anarchist, not a democrat:

I heartily accept the motto—"That government is best which governs least"; and I should like to see it acted up to more rapidly and systematically. Carried out, it finally amounts to this, which also I believe,—"That government is best which governs not at all"; and when men are prepared for it, that will be the kind of government which they will have. [4]

The day that men are so prepared will be the day that men are angels.

This antidemocratic bias is not limited to Thoreau. The Reverend William Sloane Coffin, Jr., has himself condemned democratic politics with the sweeping assertion that "as men frequently vote their ignorance, fears, and prejudices, there is never a guarantee that majority rule represents the rule of conscience." [5] And who is to determine what the rule of conscience is? It is worth noting in passing that the purpose of a democratic political system is precisely not to forge "guarantees" of morality, but to provide the mechanism by which the excesses common to any human enterprise may be corrected. Our democratic system is designed to resolve the most injustices with the most justice.

"The rule of conscience" is a nice-sounding phrase. But in the end, it only means a man's selfish desire to be at peace with himself. This peace is sought through proper and legal means by most, through improper means by some. Individual peace of mind must be given up where, in order to achieve it, an individual must flout what a majority, through a system of justice, has deemed wise.

The advocates of civil disobedience insist upon license which they would not permit to their opponents. The police, it seems, are to arrest members of the Ku Klux Klan, but not members of the Weathermen. Laws may be violated if, and only if, one is a member of the elite. As Howard Zinn has put this fantastic theory, civil disobedience would be allowed for programs of "liberal" reform, but "reactionary" civil disobedience would not be tolerated.[6] And Mr. Zinn will be the judge.

Professor Alexander M. Bickel of Yale University Law School has stated:

> If most of the things that politics is about are not seen as existing somewhere in a middle distance, well this side of moral imperatives, if they are not seen as subject on both sides of a division of opinion to fallible human choice, then the only thing left to a society is to succumb to or be seized by a dictatorship of the self-righteous. I do not wish to overstate the case, but this seems to be inevitably the conclusion to which all those disenchanted and embittered simplifiers and moralizers must come. To be revolutionary in a society like ours, is to be totalitarian, or not to know what one is doing.[7]

And what is the justification advanced for the extraordinary doctrine? My conscience, says the Reverend William Sloane Coffin, Jr., tells me that I am right. My opponents are wrong. My conscience tells me that I am on the side of the angels. My opponents are not. Therefore, I can ignore society's laws, although my opponents can claim no such privilege.

The answer to this claim is simple. The Reverend William Sloane Coffin, Jr., and his conscience may be right on any given subject and his opponents may be wrong. But if he is right, the way to demonstrate that fact is by the use of rational argument. If he can persuade a majority of his fellow citizens that he is right, his view will prevail.

Professor Alexander M. Bickel has pointed out that the fabric of society is held together by agreement on means, which are equally available or foreclosed to all. . . . When whole bushels of desires and objectives are conceived as moral imperatives, then, of course, it is natural to seek their achievement by any means. There is no need to fear that the same means will be open for use by others, because the objectives of those others are bad and unacceptable whatever the means used to attain them. And then government in freedom and an open society are impossible.[8]

Another major vice in the theory of civil disobedience is the terrible threat of zealotry and self-righteousness. This theory is inhumane, selfish, bigoted and arrogant. It claims that most members of the citizenry should be dominated and subdued because they are irredeemably benighted and incapable of comprehending the truth. They must, therefore, be redeemed by a self-anointed elite.

These doctrines of civil disobedience have been eroding our civilization in recent years. In action they have led to what I call brinkmanship. In other words, they have encouraged people to express discontent—with the system, with the laws, with government officials and policies, and with ideas—by organizing mass groups that create the potential for violence and law-breaking. This severely strains the necessary function of social order almost to the breaking point. Even when no law-breaking or violence occurs, this tactic damages the social system. It generates hostility and heated emotions, it introduces a mob psychology into our politics, and it produces very few rational insights into our problems. It produces a stress situation that no free society can long tolerate. The politics of the last six years have clearly demonstrated this. Politics have become less rational, slogans have replaced arguments, and people have become ever more concerned about order per se, without regard to its quality.

It has been suggested that nonviolence provides a socially acceptable method of political action. Many see nonviolence as a panacea. But nonviolent civil disobedience all too frequently entails violence. The Reverend William Sloane Coffin, Jr., himself stated in a previous debate in this series that nonviolent action was necessarily accompanied by a "certain amount of fringe violence."[9] Thus begins a strange rationale that violence is socially acceptable.

The excuse is sometimes offered that American history is violent or, as one extraordinary statement put it, "Violence is as American as cherry pie!" But to argue that a violent past presages, let alone justifies, a violent future is manifestly absurd. Violence is evil, and its historical existence does not remotely justify it for the future. All this used to be considered well settled, before the new barbarians arose within our gates.

The advocates of civil disobedience also purport to justify their violence on pragmatic grounds. They say that violence works. I vigorously dispute this claim. The fact is that violence has costs which its advocates do not even stop to evaluate, if indeed they know they exist. They never ask themselves whether progress could not be achieved at much less social and human cost. The effects of violence have been nothing short of tragic in every instance where violence has been employed. The burned-out areas of Watts, Detroit, Washington and Chicago provide eloquent witness of that

24

tragedy. And who can measure the invisible costs of polarization, fear and hatred?

Civil disobedience accordingly appeals to those aspects of human nature which are basest and most easily aroused. Violence is not unnatural to man. The baser aspect of human nature crosses all lines of race, religion, geography, color and national origin. As Dr. David A. Hamburg of Stanford University has recently written: "In short, aggressive behavior between man and animals, between man and man, and between groups of men, has been easily learned, practiced in play, encouraged by custom, and rewarded by most human societies for many thousands and even millions of years. . . ."[10] And Dr. Alfred A. Messer, professor of psychiatry at Emory University, has said: "But consider the nature of the human condition. Mankind is given to fits of impulsivity and wild emotions. During an angry rage, the line between verbal expression and physical action may be very thin."[11]

Today the problem of violence is an even more serious one because we are a dense urban society. We live at each other's elbows. Violence is far more costly in such a setting. The electronic media spread the image of any public violence across our nation in hours. Violence can then spread like wildfire, and it has. Thus, if anything, more civility is needed rather than less.

In a world of increasing complexity, where the problems become ever more difficult, the new barbarians do not help us with their infantile cries for instant solutions. Their tactics appeal not to man's higher reason but to his savage nature. Assassinations, bombings, intimidation, coercion, confrontations, political terrorism, insult and kidnapping give us no basis for human discourse, let alone agreement. They can only lead to polarization—the enemy of the pluralistic society, the unique human conglomerate that is America.

As I bring these remarks to a close, I must acknowledge my profound debt to one of the great intellects of our time. Father John Courtney Murray, whose death came much too early, warned of the new barbarians with an insight based on his supreme scholarship and his vast knowledge of the human condition. I can do no more than pass on to you a few thoughts gathered from the immense collection of insights contained in his works:

> Today the barbarian is the man who makes open and explicit the rejection of the traditional role of reason and logic in human affairs. He is the man who reduces all spiritual and moral questions to the test of practical results or to an analysis of language or to decision in terms of individual subjective feeling.[12]

> The barbarian need not appear in bearskins with a club in hand. He may wear a Brooks Brothers suit and carry a ball-point pen with which to write his advertising copy. In fact, even beneath the academic gown there may lurk a child of the wilderness, untutored in the high tradition of civility, who goes busily and happily about his work, a domesticated and law-abiding man, engaged in the construction of a philosophy to put an end to all philosophy, and thus put an end to the possibility of a vital consensus and to civility itself. This is perennially the work of the barbarian, to undermine rational standards of judgment. . . .[13]

The present struggle, then, is not a new one. It is merely a variant of the age-old conflict between the barbarian and civilization. The only difference is that now it is the barbarian who claims to be advanced. I submit to you that it is therefore particularly necessary to keep distinctions clear. In an age of barbarism, it is perennially the duty of civil men to create that just order which finds its truest expression in civil society. This is our task.

REBUTTALS

WILLIAM SLOANE COFFIN, JR.

I wonder if you truly believe, Morris, that rational persuasion is the best way to persuade people to be rational. Has a rational mind ever been a match for an irrational will?

Was it not terribly difficult for Gandhi and Nehru to get the idea across to the British people that what they were doing in India was a terrible thing? Gandhi and Nehru tried to persuade them, but the people of England didn't want to listen. They wrote articles, but the people didn't want to read them.

So what do you do when people don't want to pay attention and in fact will even make a great effort to subvert your efforts to attract their attention?

Or think of those monks in Vietnam who turned themselves into flaming signposts pointing at the horrors of the war, and how the average American said only, "Look at the kooky monk."

It is difficult to clear up people's doubts but even more difficult to arouse their hearts. The basic problem is to get people to care. Most people want peace at any price, as long as the peace is theirs and someone else is paying the price. I submit to you that the problem is not fundamentally one of rationally persuading people to be rational, but of getting them to care.

This is what Gandhi understood so beautifully. It wasn't until Gandhi began to engage in civil disobedience that he really began to gain the attention of a great number of Britishers, who had not paid any attention up to then. In other words, it was the suffering of the Indians which moved the British. The reasoning of Gandhi could do little before the Indians' suffering had engaged their hearts.

Gandhi knew, of course, that a conflict arouses many animosities on both sides of the issue. Resentments and grievances are both born and nourished. Therefore, if he was to persuade the British to be rational about what he was saying, he had to reduce their animosity. And he did so in two very important ways.

First, he said, "We the oppressed will accept greater suffering than we will inflict on our oppressors." That moved the British in the same way that it moved the white community in this country to see the Blacks in Montgomery or in Greensboro, take suffering upon themselves. Hearts were moved; then minds began to work.

The second thing Gandhi did was to say to the British, "We don't believe that you as individuals are evil. It's the system in which you are involved that is evil." So there was much less of the self-righteousness and moralism which you very properly criticize.

Martin Luther King followed Gandhi's lead in saying: "We are not attacking whites. We are attacking a system in which white men happen to take part, but we are attacking it as much for their sake as for our own." In other words, he de-personalized his antipathies while personalizing his sympathies.

We are still, you might say, at the Edison stage of understanding nonviolence in this country. It takes much work and a tremendous amount of commitment. But when nonviolence is understood, I think it is both an attitude and a justifiable type of operation. Its design is not so much to break the law as to uphold a higher law; not to put people on the spot, but to point out the injustice of the system in which all people are involved. And if you accept the consequences of your actions, are you not in fact upholding rather than subverting the law? I really don't think you can accuse people who engage in civil disobedience and then accept the consequences of their actions of being anarchists. Socrates was hardly an anarchist in saying "I love my city but I will not stop preaching that which I believe is true. You may kill me, but I will obey God rather than you."

Once again, our fundamental problem is how to move the hearts of people so that their minds will then go to work. Those of us who do not suffer injustices have a hard time recognizing the physical and mental hardships they have.

It is interesting, Morris, that you did not mention the war, nor the sufferings that a lot of people are enduring because of it—Indochinese as well as Americans. You did not mention Blacks, who, Lord knows, have been reasoning with the American public since the Civil War. Rationally we know that racial discrimination is evil, but we still haven't succeeded in eliminating it from our society. Too many white hearts remain unmoved.

Our dilemma is poignant. On the one hand, we have to accept the fact that moral suasion alone is not going to persuade the white community to accept Blacks on an equal basis. On the other hand, we have to recognize that violence would only exacerbate the animosities and the resentments of the whites, because violence from a small minority of

Blacks would not be strong enough to carry the battle. So somewhere between naked violence and moral suasion we have to find the route.

I am saying that we are presented with a far greater dilemma, Morris, than I think you want to recognize. Most people are not about to abandon their personal privileges for the public good. When it comes to our personal interests, we are not motivated by love of truth but by fear or even hatred of truth. And what is emotionally rooted is not intellectually soluble.

That is a good starting point for this discussion.

MORRIS I. LEIBMAN

I think that Bill has raised two important points in his remarks, points that seem to be typical of the general debate on this issue. First, he makes the remark, "It is interesting, Morris, that you did not mention the war. . . . You did not mention Blacks. . . ." Second, he says that we must "get people to care"—that we must arouse people's hearts or emotions. Let's consider these points.

I did not discuss the war in Vietnam or the Blacks in my opening statement because this debate is about civil disobedience. These days, however, it seems that the war is the universal cause of all our problems. It is the current fad and popular demonology to blame every evil that exists in contemporary America, with perhaps the exception of teenage acne, on the war in Vietnam. In preparing for this debate I resolved not to obscure the topic with an irrelevant discussion of Vietnam. Any discussion of that war is extraneous to the rather clearcut philosophical question of civil disobedience and its relationship to justice. Furthermore, a rational discussion of Vietnam would easily require as much time as this total debate. If Bill is interested, I would be happy to debate him on this separate subject at another time.

Having said that, let me make just one observation on the subject that is certainly not intended as the ultimate "truth" about Vietnam. I couldn't possibly discuss the war in Vietnam without examining the foreign policies of Wilson, Roosevelt,

Truman, Eisenhower, Kennedy and Johnson, who, as humanitarians, had the support of the people who cared and were concerned for justice in their times. These concerned men recognized that the truly concerned person must be as concerned about the victims of aggression as he is about the hapless victims of a complex war. A bleeding heart should also bleed for those murdered by the North Vietnamese.

As to my failure to mention Blacks in my opening statement, or for that matter Jews, or Spanish-speaking Americans, or American Indians or any other minority group, I want to say first that it is no secret that I am a Jew. My father lived in a Russian ghetto and my mother lived in a Polish ghetto. And for more than 20 years of my life I lived in an "American ghetto," because I lived in Polish, Italian, Black and mixed neighborhoods.

I spent almost four years of my life as chairman of the President's Poverty Council, working with Hy Bookbinder here and others on the poverty program. We suffered the dilemmas, the frustrations, the agonies of America—the world's first conglomerate that took Lebanese, Jews, Poles, Irish, Chinese, English and many other ethnic groups. America took them all, with their historical problems and prejudices and their animosities, and it is trying to make a just society in one place. I don't think we fully appreciate the enormity of the task, the greatness of the American achievement.

I did not mention these facts or bring up the subject of Blacks or other minorities before because it seems to me pernicious to relate respect for the law, the quality of one's citizenship, and the commitment to democracy and reason to one's race or national origin or religion. Sure I'm a Jew and a product of the ghetto. But is that what is important about me? I am first of all a human being. Every Jew or Black or Catholic or German or Indian is first of all a human being, with a spirit and a mind. The great horrors of the twentieth century have been provoked by those who were more concerned over a man's race than over the fact that he was a man.

So, Bill, I didn't mention anything about Blacks earlier because the great issues of this debate are about people, all people. And all people are entitled to the same rules and rights and are bound by the same responsibilities. This is our topic.

It is very destructive to the free, humane society to say that just because a man is Irish he should be excused for hating the British, or just because he is Black he should be less bound by the law, since the law formerly discriminated against Blacks. In truth a member of any and every minority must revere the law, if anything, even more than the members of the majority. The most important and basic function of law is the protection of minority rights within our system. The threat from civil disobedience, in view of recent history, is far greater to minorities than to majorities.

And now for Bill's second point, that we must "get people to care" and "arouse the hearts and emotions" to "*provoke* change." This appeal to the hearts disturbs me. I see a past in which Russian Cossacks and German storm troopers were very emotional; their hearts not their minds were aroused, and we can find their equals in other times and in every country. Arousing of the heart, of the emotions and passions, of hate and enthusiasm, loose an unreasoning beast, Bill. I fear this beast because it has done so much damage and evil in this century. We must always remember that those with whom we disagree have the same rights, in America, as we do. They may become the majority. Is it more comforting to think of a reasonable majority or one of aroused emotions? A non-rational, emotional minority can do enough damage to a society. We don't need emotional, aroused majorities. We need reason and civility.

Take a recent lesson from England. It saddens me to think how poorly and immaturely the England that I respect, that was the birthplace of my law, handled its Black problem the minute it had more than a few Blacks. What happened to this mature, homogeneous, law-loving, just society? I merely cite this to show the complexity of social problems. They are full of dilemmas that cannot be resolved by simple emotional positions. They can only be solved through reason and a commitment on all sides to work together, and this means within commonly agreed upon rules.

How many thousands of years has it taken men to produce a free, democratic civilization committed to reason? To go about talking about "arousing emotions" is to flirt with the destruction of the whole edifice of civilization. The advanced society that backs away from reason sinks into a far worse barbarism than the primitive society that has not yet embraced reason. We tend to escape the choice by creating escape-lands, utopias. In doing this we should be very aware of one key thing: America has been the place, the only real place, to escape to for almost 500 years. It has been the continent where people sought and found a juster and better and freer life. And it was not a utopia, is not a utopia. We must remember—both in pride and realism—that we have done so much in America, that we have such real and rational opportunities.

America is a real live land of hope because it is based on a system of justice set up by men who knew all too well the passions and aroused emotions of the Old World. They understood the evils that zealotry, fanaticism and persecution had wreaked in Europe. So they resolved to eliminate that passion and emotion from our society by creating a system that sought to resolve conflict through a rational, democratic process, using discussion, compromise and debate. This system cannot afford the moral arrogance of those who claim that they *know* absolutely what is moral and when the majority or the government is immoral.

Our system takes great self-discipline. It takes effort to be civil. A society based on reason and discussion can't function without a high degree of civility and mutual respect between opponents. Our forefathers understood that to "sell" love is possible, but that doing so is much harder and more frustrating than selling hate. Hate can be created by provoking and arousing. Love can only be created by understanding, and it requires thought and true commitment.

In these days of danger to and disenchantment with our system on the part of some, I still believe in the melting pot, the pluralistic society, the society of minority rights, the ideas of individual rights and conscience. That is why I so strongly feel that civil disobedience, uncivil behavior and brinkmanship are all great threats. They undermine minority rights and the legitimate claims of conscience by supplanting process and procedure with arrogant force. When persuasion and the system of democratic laws are abandoned the first to suffer are always the minorities and the dissenters. That is why they should be in the forefront of those who condemn civil disobedience.

A pluralistic society that recognizes individual rights and the claims of conscience requires a system of rules that says to us all: Don't decide the issues or resolve the frictions according to what your emotions tell you, or what your heritage or your language or your ancestry tells you, try instead to be a new kind of man who uses reason and persuasion.

As we consider this issue of civil disobedience, let us not become bogged down in the endless excuses for disobedience. These rationalizations and apologies include the war in Vietnam, discrimination against minorities, the fact that we live in a violent and irrational world with a violent and irrational past, poverty, injustice, actions and mistakes by individual officeholders, imperfections in the democratic process, lies told to the public, the "need" to be heard or understood or paid attention to, the difficulty of progress, the many setbacks to justice, the moral righteousness of *the* cause, and many other such similar pleadings. These are all cop-outs. Those who are concerned about such problems should follow the proper multiple procedures our system affords to those who have the determination and fortitude to really care about their cause. But they should realize that this takes work.

I am glad Bill admitted in his opening statement that civil disobedience is at times a hindrance to justice. This admission, in my view, unveils the key flaw in the whole argument for civil disobedience. Who is to decide when it is "good" and when it is "bad"? It makes of civil disobedience the tool of the arrogant, those who would put their will above the law laid down by society when they don't get their way. There can be no excuse for using such a tactic or for the arrogance of those who claim they are more moral than the "unenlightened majority." There is no excuse for using force to make this "unenlightened majority" care. If the majority really doesn't care, then only through reason and civility can they be made to share the caring, to embrace the ideal of saving humanity and the commitment to higher justice that they are accused of lacking. In an open society we must always choose reason rather than force as our means. Thus, I hope Bill's commitment to reason is stronger than his comment—"Has a rational mind ever been a match for an irrational will?"—would indicate. The answer I give is that of course it has! That is why man has progressed from savagery to a point where we can rationally argue about what is needed to produce *more* justice and civility.

If we do see a dilemma in our system between obedience to law and our moral values, or if there is not room for proper individual action or dissent, then let's modify the system as we have continually done in the past. The system was designed to be modified, and in fact has been radically altered through legal means a number of times in our history. Let's not throw temper tantrums and proclaim the system is rotten whenever we don't get our way. Too often that is the childish attitude one finds among the civil disobedients and others whose real problem is that they do not understand the American system of law and justice. Let's take care not to destroy

41

the system that provides the only framework for achievement. I choose reason over emotion—and people who care with their minds and not their prejudices.

DISCUSSION

HYMAN BOOKBINDER, American Jewish Committee: I am having trouble thus far in the discussion because we are dealing with this abstraction called civil disobedience. I am not sure I know what we are talking about. If we are talking about a general principle to the effect that people and groups have the right to decide which laws to follow, obviously society cannot sanction that. If we are justifying particular instances in the past, that may be something else.

But I would like to ask Dr. Coffin this: recognizing that we are dealing with a tactic that is delicate and dangerous—one which could bring down the very system itself—what are your criteria for access to this very delicate and difficult instrument?

DR. COFFIN: What you are asking is a very, very difficult thing to answer.

As a rule you would not engage in civil disobedience as a first resort, or as a second resort, but only as a last resort—having written your congressmen, having visited senators time and time again. In protesting the war many of us went through these legal procedures again and again, with breathtaking lack of success. Several senators said to me, "You won't believe it, Reverend, but most of us around here are watching the plaster break up on the ceiling and trying to figure out how we can be over there instead of here when it all caves in."

MR. BOOKBINDER: But didn't the non-civil disobedient tactic of the '68 elections do much more in this field than what you call civil disobedience?

DR. COFFIN: I'm not saying civil disobedience does everything. I'm just saying it's one tactic among many. And I guess I would like to add that it is one way of maintaining self-respect. If you can't change the system, at least you can make sure the system doesn't change you.

ROBERT GORALSKI, moderator of the debate: Mr. Leibman, would you care to comment on Mr. Bookbinder's question?

MR. LEIBMAN: First, on the acceptance of consequences. I treated that in my paper. The fact is that most of those who practice civil disobedience don't want to accept the consequences. That is why you have "mass civil disobedience," so that the law is not able to impose the consequences. The anonymity of the mob protects them. Then there are pleas for amnesty, and all sorts of other devices. And when they are arrested, and the police try to take them into custody, they resist or go limp or flee, and the stage is set for violence and brutality.

So I treat that question in the paper. I think the fact is that it is the rare case where a Martin Luther King accepts the consequences.

Let's also eliminate the question of test cases or testing. That too is treated in my paper. Testing a law is not civil disobedience. Testing is following the processes. And we wouldn't have to have a court system if there was not inherent in the whole system the special right to test the validity of laws.

DR. COFFIN: In other words, you have to break it, Morris, to test it.

MR. LEIBMAN: Yes.

DR. COFFIN: That's a funny thing about the American system. You have to break a law to find out if it's legal.

MR. LEIBMAN: That's a special right—a special method, the only method we know, for testing a law so that it isn't tested in a moot fashion. It's a special part of our system. We say, "If you violate it and want to appeal it, you have all your rights." This is a procedure, however, that can and should be effected by one violation, committed by one person. It is designed for new laws or laws that have become uncertain in the light of changed circumstances.

So we have created this unique system where more people can constantly test their consciences or their injustices or their prejudices than has ever been possible under any other kind of system. We talk about an "over-lawed" society. The fact is that we have the "over-lawed" society because ours is the first society in which human beings have had such rights.

Let me say just one thing about the war. The real question is: who is going to decide what war you want to be in? Again we have methods. I am going to shock the Reverend Coffin by saying that at the time the American people don't want the war, they won't have it. There have been a whole series of myths here about immorality, illegality, et cetera. But, although it was never publicized, the Reverend Coffin knows how recent it was that every college poll showed approval of the war. College opinion polls!

The question of what is the majority will is the subject for another debate. Certainly when we fight in Korea because of "the UN," I would like to have some standards about that too, and about whether the world conscience is measured by the UN.

Getting back to the issue Mr. Bookbinder raised, I am glad to have the Reverend Coffin say, at least, that civil disobedience should be used as a last resort. But we still have the question, "Who decides what is the last resort?" Now, if we recognize civil disobedience as so dangerous that it should be used only as a last resort, then I would like to know what are the last resort situations, and who decides them. Does the other side have the same right, and where do you get the right to decide on the proper time dimension?

DR. COFFIN: I think the only questions a man can ask are "How great is the evil which I oppose? Have I exhausted all legal remedies? Or is the evil so great that I have no time for these? What will be the consequences of my action on other people, now or later?" These are the kinds of very difficult questions which I think you have to ask yourself.

And I think, finally, there is no easy answer. But you have to make a decision. Otherwise, you surrender your conscience to the state—and that is very bad democracy, as well as very bad religion.

MR. LEIBMAN: I argue that you don't surrender your conscience to the state by obeying the law, because I would contend that with respect to the race issue, the Black issue, the issue of Soviet Jews, it's the disobedients who have interfered with progress, who have hindered justice and solutions. They have made for polarization, they have made for hatreds and angers. Problem-solving is the only way to go forward. I would say the Supreme Court has done more for Black rights and poverty rights than Watts and Chicago and Detroit and Washington did. Take a look at the ruins.

MICHAEL BERNSTEIN, Committee on Education and Labor, U.S. House of Representatives: I am a little bit disturbed by some of the exemplars that Dr. Coffin refers to as justifying his position. His remarks indicate that he does look outside himself for authority, even though it is moral authority. And I think that he has been inaccurate in his references to some of his sources.

First of all, if Martin Luther King was simply testing the law, then there was no need for everybody else to disobey it, because all you need is one person to disobey a law in order to get the test. If he went beyond that, then he was engaged in what we would call unjustified civil disobedience.

Now, it happens that I think the law in this particular case was an unjust law. I think it was unconstitutional, even if the Supreme Court didn't say so. But I am willing to be bound by the law in this kind of society.

There are the other cases, for example, Antigone. Antigone didn't go around asking for help to break the law. She didn't say to the other people, "This is an unjust law, disobey it." She disobeyed it, nobody else did. Her sister wanted to join her, but she refused her sister's help. She took this disobedience upon herself. And Socrates, whom you mentioned, didn't ask anybody to disobey the law either. He went through Athens preaching that the laws and the customs were bad, but he didn't say they should be disobeyed. And when he was convicted and condemned to death and his friends came to him and said, "We'll help you to escape," he said, "I refuse to escape because I obey the law." That's what Socrates said. So we have a few exemplars who refute your position.

On the matter of conscience, I think your opponent didn't go the whole way. There is a place for conscience, but it is in the individual. There is no group conscience any more than there is group thought. Conscience is an individual thing. A person who feels that a law is unjust, even though it may have been properly enacted, even though it's constitutional and valid, may disobey it. But he doesn't tell other people to disobey it. He tells them to use the processes of society to change it.

This business of a collective conscience or a universal conscience is taking an abstraction like man in the mass and treating it as if it were a single organism with a single mind, a single heart and a single soul. People often do this and it really doesn't make any sense. It's completely untrue. Even a crowd of a hundred people is a hundred consciences, not one conscience.

DR. COFFIN: Doesn't it strike you that men finally have more in common than they have in conflict? I mean, what we have between us that's different is nothing compared to what we have that binds us all together in the human fold, and I wouldn't exclude conscience from among the things that bind us. We have appetites which bind us together but we also have conscience. Now I agree with you—in the final analysis, conscience is an individual matter. But I think people's consciences, when aroused, generally will tell them that, for instance, racial discrimination is wrong.

MR. BERNSTEIN: Now, wait a minute.

DR. COFFIN: In this country.

MR. BERNSTEIN: You can arouse the conscience of your neighbor when you think the law's an unjust one, even though it's a valid one in a democratic system by telling him what's wrong with the law and saying, "I refuse to obey it."

DR. COFFIN: Right.

MR. BERNSTEIN: Let others draw their own conclusions.

DR. COFFIN: Right.

MR. BERNSTEIN: If their consciences are touched, then, as individuals, they will refuse to obey it. But you don't have the right to say to them, "Disobey this law."

DR. COFFIN: This is what King was doing in Birmingham. Blacks as a group—

MR. BERNSTEIN: Then he wasn't testing? He was doing more than testing?

DR. COFFIN: That's right. Are you saying you don't think he was right?

MR. BERNSTEIN: No, I said that I think he was right because this happens to be a law which is clearly wrong in terms of even our own Constitution and the Fourteenth Amendment, which requires—

DR. COFFIN: Right, but he didn't wait for it to go all the way up to the Supreme Court.

MR. BERNSTEIN: Maybe he would have even been wiser if he had.

DR. COFFIN: Well, I don't know. Why should a bunch of Blacks wait around forever and ever before getting employment?

MR. BERNSTEIN: Don't say forever. Do you think that every improvement in American society was the result of civil disobedience?

51

DR. COFFIN: No, but we're talking about Birmingham.

MR. BERNSTEIN: Yes, but then what you're doing is conceding that there can be progress without civil disobedience.

DR. COFFIN: Oh, of course. I concede that right away.

HERBERT MILLER, Georgetown University Law Center: Mr. Leibman, you have given me a vision and the vision is of people like you and me sitting around in an air-conditioned room and having reasoned discourse while the bombs drop on people who cannot, under any circumstances, reasonably discourse with us—while our law enforcement apparatus and our courts are sentencing young people and Blacks to barbaric sentences in a prison system that is only destructive. You're suggesting that we must go on reasonably discoursing while the minds, the bodies, the spirits of these people are being destroyed.

Are you saying therefore, that there's no place for more than the reasoned discourse you're talking about—no matter what the circumstances, no matter how outrageous the injustice?

MR. LEIBMAN: I have still to be shown the instance where the kind of injustices you're talking about cannot be handled by our processes. I think Jefferson pointed out years ago, with his great vision, the need for education—the need for constantly lifting the human mind—in order to get individuals talking about a social conscience rather than personal convenience or what's good or what's easy for them.

I think today more than anywhere at any time in history there are thousands of lawyers like you and me working around-the-clock, day and night, in the ghettos, in the community action programs, in the courts, in the police courts, making monumental historical progress. We've gotten a whole new dimension of social justice that's amplified year by year with the Civil Rights Act, with the Civil Rights Commission, and with a succession of court decisions. I think that if you look around you'd be amazed at how many people are not just sitting in air-conditioned offices talking, but who are doing the job that has to be done.

I would urge one other thing. One of my problems in talking to law students arises when they say to me, "How much time off do you give us for a poverty program or to go out into the ghetto?" I say "None. I don't want you to go out there ignorant, superficial, supercilious. I don't want you to go out there unless you *care*, as the Reverend Coffin says. Do it the way I do it, 16 and 18 hours a day, including Saturdays and Sundays. That will help make a lawyer out of you, that will help make a problem solver out of you, but please don't go out into that area if it doesn't really beat within you. And you know you have to do it because if you don't, you won't be any damned good."

DR. COFFIN: Mr. Leibman. With all due respect, we've had Civil Rights Commission report after Civil Rights Commission report, Supreme Court opinion after Supreme Court opinion. Yet, for the last decade or two, there's been damned little change. The same people are being raped by our society and, as a lawyer, as one who has tried to use professional skills to participate at the citizens' level to change this system politically, are you not beginning to have doubts about the power of reasonable discourse?

MR. LEIBMAN: You and I then evaluate the perspective differently. Let me give the other side of the coin. When we talk about Martin Luther King, I think of the man's agony at a few places like Watts, when he was there. And remember when he was shot in the leg, and he said, "What's happened? My God, we mustn't let this happen!" He understood that the unleashing of violence would destroy what had been accomplished and that it offered no substitute.

Beware of the bombastic rhetoric and the violence. As Hitler's radio chief used to say, "That's how we get the lightning." Lots of rhetoric and lots of violence.

I say that this is a time not for disobedience but for a higher civility. The challenge to us is the challenge inherent in the American system. Here is the only place where you can appeal to men's minds and if we don't win humanity in men's minds, we're not going to win it in their hearts.

LAWRENCE SPEISER, attorney, formerly with American Civil Liberties Union: I'm having difficulty with Mr. Leibman's and Dr. Coffin's definitions of civil disobedience.

Mr. Leibman suggested Watts as an example of civil disobedience. I don't think it is in any way an example of civil disobedience. I'm puzzled by his using it as an example.

And, Dr. Coffin, I think you are right to say that neither testing a law nor breaking a law that's already been found to be unconstitutional is civil disobedience. I would think a better definition of civil disobedience is breaking a law of unquestionable constitutionality and legality in order to dramatize a moral issue. A good example would be where people sit down in the middle of an intersection. They aren't challenging the legality of the traffic law or the prohibition

54

on obstructing traffic; they are doing something in order to attract attention. Now that, it seems to me, would be civil disobedience. They can't question the constitutionality of the law but they are attempting to dramatize something. The situation would seem to me to fit your ultimate criterion—that after you've tried everything else, you would engage in that.

Now, does that square with your definition?

DR. COFFIN: Not quite, at the level of motivation. I don't think everybody who commits civil disobedience does it in order to attract attention. You see, I think ultimately in this world you have to do what's right and penultimately you have to do what's effective. One of the sicknesses of American society is that we have these reversed so that the ultimate question is always: Will I be effective? And that's one of our problems today—we're not that concerned with being right.

I think in a strange way Socrates was very effective because he didn't care that much about being effective. When they handed him the hemlock, he didn't say, "Wait a minute, boys, is Plato going to write me up?" [Laughter.] And Thoreau wasn't that concerned with being effective, or Nathan Hale, or many of our heroes. They're effective. They reach us. They move us because they were concerned with what's right, and they weren't constantly trying to be prudent, constantly trying to be effective in one thing or another.

So it's on the level of motivation that I would disagree with you. Otherwise I think what you say about civil disobedience is right.

Let me get back to Watts for a brief moment, because I think it represents a very special kind of civil disobedience.

55

It was less planned and more an outbreak of despair—a riot that came from discouragement and a feeling of being trampled under with nothing happening, as the gentleman there was suggesting.

But I think, Morris, that one would have to say that there had been study after study after study of the conditions in Watts and nothing was done until Watts exploded. That's why that Black went up to Martin Luther King and said, "Reverend King, here's our manifesto," and he struck a match and put it under King's nose and said, "And we know and you know it works." The fact of the matter is that in the case of Watts it did work. People began to pay a lot more attention to Watts. It is a sad commentary that after Watts blew up, and probably because people were scared, they felt it was time to make some concessions.

Now if Watts had burst out and its citizens had attacked Orange County or had invaded Los Angeles, then the backlash might have been so great as to impede justice. But I don't think you can say the Watts riot did not help the advance of justice—though still to only a very pitiful degree.

WILLIAM STANMEYER, Law School, Georgetown University: A question for both the participants. Dr. Ernest Van Den Haag, in a recent article written for the *Encyclopaedia Britannica* on civil disobedience, asserts that the disobedient claims a universality to his conscience, that he sees right not only as right for him but as right for all men. The disobedient asserts, in effect, that the other people in the public dialogue are wrong and thus should not follow their consciences. Thus, he seems inclined, in the practical world, to attempt to inflict the decision of his conscience on the others. So we have members of SDS [Students for a Democratic Society] on college campuses who say the draft is wrong for me, I won't be drafted, and I will prevent the Marine Corps from recruiting others on campus.

Now I'd like to ask first Dr. Coffin if he ever counseled students not to let their own moralism inflict itself on others, if he ever tries to help them make these distinctions—or don't they need to?

DR. COFFIN: I agree, you can't trample on other people's consciences in the name of your own. That's a contradiction. At the same time, it is important that the truth to which you witness should be as true for the other fellow as it is for you. Gandhi used to say, "All confrontations should be considered as occasions for all men to rise above their present condition." Dealing with the manufacturers of India, he was trying to say that the truth to which the workers were trying to witness was true for the manufacturers, as well. King was saying the same thing to whites.

MR. LEIBMAN: May I return? Apparently each of us gets a chance to surrebut in this. The problem I have is that once you subjectivize the conscience and say we all can go our way like bugs in a pond, then I don't see why the parents in Richmond can't wave their version of that match you just waved in our faces metaphorically at Watts in the face of the drivers of school buses and say, "We too will follow our conscience to the ultimate degree because we too have a right to do that, regardless of your feeling." How do you answer the problem of the parent who thinks Judge Merhige is mistaken?

DR. COFFIN: That's why I talked at the beginning about means and ends. I didn't say the end justifies the means, Morris, but I don't know what else justifies the means if not the end. [Laughter.] But the means must be commensurate with the end or the end will no longer be realizable. But the end is what's important. Why would the parents in Richmond, Virginia, be waving the match? If you hold that justice is the ultimate rational goal of the society, then you have to say, "Well, who's trying to move society in the direction of justice and who is trying to protect privileges and deny justice to those folks who don't have it now?"

The busing situation can be pretty complicated but basically those parents, I think, are really trying to protect the interest of their own more-privileged children as against the interest of less-privileged children who are involved in this busing thing. I think that's why I say you have to take the end seriously.

If you start infringing on the civil liberties of somebody else, by opposing busing or by blocking the door of a ROTC building, then, of course, it's a different situation. Then you have to have further justification.

MR. BOOKBINDER: On that very point, might I ask Dr. Coffin then, would you then disapprove of the May Day demonstrations of last year?

DR. COFFIN: In Washington?

MR. BOOKBINDER: Yes.

DR. COFFIN: Most certainly.

MR. BOOKBINDER: You would?

DR. COFFIN: Yes. I think the way the police behaved was civil disobedience at its worst. [Laughter.] I mean, the police came charging down on their scooters and in their cars at a reckless speed.

MR. BOOKBINDER: That's very cute and very clever but I won't—

DR. COFFIN: No, it's very serious, sir.

MR. BOOKBINDER: I'm asking whether you would, in light of what you just said, disapprove of a demonstration, the purposes of which were, one, to dramatize the war in Vietnam by depriving many hundreds of thousands of other citizens of their civil rights and liberties.

DR. COFFIN: Right.

MR. BOOKBINDER: Would you, therefore, disapprove of that kind of civil disobedience?

DR. COFFIN: I'll answer that question if you'll let me get back to the civil disobedience of John Mitchell and the police department. Okay?

MR. BOOKBINDER: You can talk about any other subject you want but let's just stay with my subject first.

DR. COFFIN: My problem was not so much with the action as with the explanation of the actions. Nonviolence is really trying to speak truth to power, but Rennie Davis engaged in the language of power more than he did the language of truth. He said, "We're going to shut down Washington." Now, if I'd been Rennie Davis, I'd have said, "We're not going to shut down Washington, everybody knows that we can never shut down Washington. This is a pathetic little group trying to block a little bit of traffic. Why do we do it? To plead with you who have the power to put it at the service of the truth we're trying to witness to, because

59

we think you know that it's as true for you as it is for us that this war is a criminal war."

If he had spoken in that language, you see, it would have been a different thing. Later he proclaimed, "We're going to take the Congress hostage." Of course, he wasn't going to take the Congress hostage. He should have said, "We can't possibly take the Congress hostage, so why do we do a silly thing like this? Because we want to plead with congressmen, who know that this war is wrong, to stop making themselves into a Ho Chi Minh Trail over to the White House voting all the supplies the White House demands to prosecute the war."

MR. BOOKBINDER: Now may I repeat my question? [Laughter.] You had commented about Socrates not wanting to deprive anybody else of civil liberties.

DR. COFFIN: I said that nobody should have a problem with that one.

MR. BOOKBINDER: Nobody?

DR. COFFIN: With this one I can see how people would have a problem.

MR. BOOKBINDER: Oh, I see.

DR. COFFIN: And, therefore, the explanation becomes terribly important.

MR. BOOKBINDER: What's the answer, by the way?

DR. COFFIN: I don't disapprove that much of that action. What's a 10-minute traffic jam or even a half-hour's, compared to the war? But you should use the right language to try to communicate what you're doing. If you don't, then you will arouse such resentment. People will not say, "Now

I wonder why they did that and I wonder how much I've thought and read about the war."

So you have to be very careful that you don't make it a counterproductive thing by your rhetoric.

MODERATOR GORALSKI: This gentleman over here, could we get your question.

DR. COFFIN: Could I make my remarks about the police?

MODERATOR GORALSKI: Please.

DR. COFFIN: I think it's very important in any discussion of civil disobedience to recognize that the government engages in it with great regularity. This is a case in point. When police come tearing down on the demonstrators in their scooters and in their cars, where one little reckless turn, a slip of the brake would make a cop guilty of murder, that is a civilly disobedient act—particularly when it's sanctioned by those higher up who then go on to praise it.

Think of the mass arrests that were made on that day. No one was prosecuted because constitutional rights had been violated. You would have thought the President of the United States, when he came into the White House, took an oath of office to uphold the traffic of Washington, D. C. It was incredible how the traffic of Washington, D. C. became more important than the United States Constitution.

WILLIAM C. SULLIVAN, formerly assistant to the director, Federal Bureau of Investigation, now with the Crime Prevention Institute: I didn't intend to allude to this but Dr. Coffin mentioned the police bearing down upon these gentle souls. I happened to be out in that demonstration and I know of no serious injury that occurred, none at all. So the slip was not made by the officer and to allude to it is to speculate. Now may I come to a question.

DR. COFFIN: The mass arrests were made, though.

MR. SULLIVAN: What was the alternative?

DR. COFFIN: The traffic jam and that's not worse than illegal arrests on a massive scale. That's my point.

MR. SULLIVAN: Not compared with the deprivation of civil liberties. I recognize the idealism and sincerity of Dr. Coffin and I'm sure that many, if not all, of us agree upon the end of social justice to which he has referred. However, I have listened to members of the Ku Klux Klan, the Minute Men, the old Nazi Party, express the same basic thought which you have just expressed and even use some of the same words—all in the name of this higher law, their conscience. They too believe in their conscience that they are doing what is right. Therefore, don't you think that this particular course opens in the long run a Pandora's box and isn't there a better way to reach the goal that we all want to reach?

DR. COFFIN: Are you saying that we shouldn't have any Socrates?

MR. SULLIVAN: No, I didn't say that.

DR. COFFIN: Or there shouldn't be any Jesus? You see, I agree with you that it is a dilemma. But, if you back off and say, "Well, we'd better all obey the law because, if one person breaks it, that opens a Pandora's box, everybody else will start to break it," then—

It's a very interesting thing with the Ku Klux Klan. Very few of its members have overtly disobeyed the law and said, "Arrest me, I'm trying to dramatize an injustice." And even when the '64 civil rights law was passed, Maddox, I think, was the only one who closed his restaurant. All the others seemed to say, "Money is more important than conscience," and accepted integration. It was very, very—kind of cynical actually, you know, and I think that speaks to your point, Mr. Sullivan. Not everybody's going to say, "I'll take a 10-year rap because I think this thing is important."

VINCENT MacQUEENEY, Internal Security Division, Department of Justice: I'd like to say about the May Day demonstration—my division was concerned with it to some extent—that Rennie Davis had hoped to get 100,000 people. He had about 30,000 at one time in the park and then the number, due to the actions of the D. C. police in dispersing it, was reduced to about 20,000. His purpose wasn't only to block traffic but by that means, to stop the operations of the government. I think the President does have a duty to see that the government functions because the example set by this type of conduct and the idea it could be tolerated could be extremely damaging to the social fabric of society.

About the arrests, they were made with probable cause, but the action couldn't later be brought because the police could not identify those they had picked up. But I saw them arrested and picked up in the street as they were sitting in it. Dr. Coffin, I think, concedes they were blocking the streets. That's a crime, or a small misdemeanor. Even though the police were unable to identify individual offenders because they didn't have the time to take photographs and so forth, I think those arrests were valid.

But let me come to the question. I agree that social justice is a higher goal than law and order, but don't you feel that law and order is an essential condition, a sine qua non, without which you cannot have justice?

DR. COFFIN: Right. I couldn't agree more. You can't have social justice without law and order but you can have law and order with precious little social justice. That is, instead of an established order, you can have an established disorder, and many of us would agree that's probably what goes on in the Soviet Union in many areas. We don't have any quarrel with people like Solzhenitsyn doing all kinds of illegal things. We applaud such people when they send out their manuscripts illegally. We say, "Thank God there are a few alive consciences there in the Soviet Union"—the same way that we applaud a few live consciences in communist countries all over the place. But when it comes to our own country, we suddenly think, well, we must be vastly different.

MR. MacQUEENEY: Doesn't civil disobedience tend to destroy law and order, tend to undermine it, particularly with a vast underclass? I mean, when you encourage civil disobedience, aren't you encouraging the chaos we have in our cities?

DR. COFFIN: I think that most people can tell the difference between engaging in civil disobedience in order to dramatize an injustice, and breaking the law for the hell of it. There is the danger that civil disobedience will spill over, but most people recognize the rather sophisticated concept of the law in search of itself. They know the law is always trying to move along so that it may reflect a little more and reject a little less the justice which is always its goal.

MR. LEIBMAN: It is interesting to hear the full range of comments and references. They demonstrate that good intention is not virtue and, when good intention gets zealous, I think those who like social justice ought to have their antenna up and say, "Oh-oh, danger." But then the reply is, "Oh, well, a little traffic jam, a little pregnancy, a little violence and everybody knows they don't really want to stop Washington or kidnap Kissinger or blow up the crowd." But everybody doesn't know it.

As a matter of fact, there's a lot of evidence that they do want to do what they threaten and all it takes is one kook in that little crowd who thinks it's a good idea for it to happen. I don't want to let it happen. I don't want to have traffic stopped by those who are for or against abortion, for or against a tax measure, for or against Bangladesh, et cetera. I don't want those with strong views on a subject to interfere with the civil liberties of a whole society.

There is no place in our society for the notion that there is some position between civility and incivility or legality and illegality. Once you accept the notion that each person's method of attracting attention to his cause is legitimate political action, you are in an anarchistic muddle. Suddenly you have a "dirty trick society," a circus society. In the "dirty trick" or circus society, the most sneaky, the most bizarre or the most outrageous make the decisions.

In this "dirty trick society" the question on any issue becomes, "How can we get a two-headed man on our side? What bizarre action will make the greatest media impact?" Such strategies deny the idea that man will achieve social justice through his mind, through his convictions and through his continued growth and learning.

65

We are not looking for this bizarre circus world but a just and rational society. We are trying to build a society based on the unity of free and reasonable people. I don't believe this can come from irrationality or separatism. I don't want Black ghettos or Jewish ghettos or Swedish ghettos or any kind of ghettos. I don't want them policed by their own police. I don't want them making their own rules to attract attention.

I find this disturbing divisiveness even in Israel, where there are strong forces working in the direction of unity. In Israel there are 17—or is it 22?—political parties. I want something less divisive—a system for community—and I contend that nobody has come up with a better system than this miracle of America with its built-in processes for constant change, its way of organizing the hope that a common ground for community can come out of the morality, the dreams and the good intentions of individuals and groups.

DR. COFFIN: Morris, that's a fatuous statement. I'm a great believer in America—

MR. LEIBMAN: I'm entitled to one, Bill. [Laughter.]

DR. COFFIN: —but it is a country which was also founded on the blood of 10 million Indians and developed on the sweat of 40 million slaves. So let's be just a little bit humble about how great we are.

MR. LEIBMAN: That's an argument I resent because it's precisely your position that lacks humility. You are saying, it seems to me, that because there was violence against Blacks and Indians and others when this nation was built, violence by minorities today is somehow justified—a sort of two wrongs make a right theory. I think that to read the history of man is to read the history of man's inhumanity to man.

66

Those failures don't mean it's acceptable to say, "Well, look, we killed a few then, maybe we've got to kill a few now."

DR. COFFIN: That's not what I'm saying, Morris.

MR. LEIBMAN: I am against the killing and I don't accept the idea that violence is American. Violence is a part of human nature and I want something that says no to all violence.

DR. COFFIN: All right but you're also going to show yourself lacking in compassion, Morris, if you turn your back on those who are fundamentally your allies but who, out of despair, and because they've been trampled under, feel they have no other recourse but violence. Basically they're your allies because they are struggling for a better system of justice. It's like a kid with a temper tantrum who is struggling for something he has an absolute right to get but he's so despairing that he engages in a temper tantrum and you come up and say, "Oh, naughty, naughty, having a temper tantrum," and pay no attention to what it is the poor kid's after.

MR. LEIBMAN: I would like to reply to that by saying I've used the same example with gangs, the famous gangs of Chicago. I've spent days and weeks and months saying "Don't give me your temper tantrums." Incidentally, I talk to them as I do to a corporate board. "Don't pop out with that easy thing, throwing a bomb or breaking something up," I say, "I want you to understand how to use the levers of power."

DR. COFFIN: Right.

MR. LEIBMAN: I know what it's like when you work week after week and you get a restaurant going and you've got supplies and you set up a system for running it. You've finally got a business going, right out where it's been burned down, and then there's an argument about whose girlfriend's going to be the waitress and who's going to take care of the money and how we're going to keep some records and how we're going to get participation from other gang leaders. And you sit there day after day, and then this frustration explodes and this one shoots somebody and this one goes to jail and you're pleading every day: "My God, we've got to keep this going, because the other approach isn't going to work."

So don't talk about compassion and frustration to me. I say you've got to go out there and raise the level, get away from the temper tantrums, get away from the excuses, get away from the history, and say "Look, there's only one way to do it, with sweat, and we've got to do it together."

DR. COFFIN: All right, of course, you have to tell them that. But you can't—

MR. LEIBMAN: But don't say that I have no compassion.

DR. COFFIN: —blame the people for becoming irrational in the face of century-long irrationality.

MR. LEIBMAN: I don't know what to do with this, Bill, except to say, "Please, I'm going to help you try to replace your irrationality with reason."

DR. COFFIN: But if they don't listen to you, you can't turn your back on them. That's what I mean.

MR. LEIBMAN: I'm not saying turn your back.

SAMUEL McCRACKEN, Reed College: Yes, I wish I had had the foresight to bring with me tonight a copy of the Italian Fascist Party's first program. It contains about 18 impeccable goals, which I'm sure Mr. Coffin would have signed his name to without a second's thought. The problem is that nobody ever runs for office or seizes power on a platform of "Put me in power, and I will give you Auschwitz." All mass movements that work have impeccably liberal social justice goals and, if you tell me that I must evaluate ends over means, then that leaves me able to oppose only a fairly small bunch of ineffectual crazies, the KKK, the Minute Men, people of that sort, who really are no threat. Now, how do I distinguish between the people who turn out to be Nazis eventually and the people who have the truth?

DR. COFFIN: Well, I'm not sure that the Nazis didn't say who they were pretty honestly. The Aryan theory was spelled out fairly completely. What you say though is probably correct. In my effort to get the emphasis away from the nicety or the ugliness of method and to focus it on the goal, maybe I haven't talked enough about the method. I certainly agree that means are—perhaps you could say—ends in the process of becoming.

MR. LEIBMAN: Exactly.

DR. COFFIN: You cannot talk about the brotherhood of man and use class warfare as a means without being involved in some kind of untenable situation.

MR. BOOKBINDER: But if there are no ends, there are only means in life.

DR. COFFIN: Come on now, there are ends. But I think the moral emphasis is not only on the means. Very often the means is a political pragmatic type of consideration and the moral justification is what you're trying to aspire to.

MR. MacQUEENEY: Would society tolerate a tantrum on any large level? I claim that it cannot and it will not, regardless of what argument you have. It will not tolerate a temper tantrum by a large group.

DR. COFFIN: I think the United States population is watching the United States government engage in an enormous temper tantrum in Southeast Asia, and I think they've taken it very nicely.

JAMES CARY, Copley News Service: I've been sitting here jotting down some of the absolutes that the Reverend Coffin has been using: social justice, morality, higher goal, good, right, wrong, truth. I'd like to ask you why you feel that you're qualified to judge what these things are?

DR. COFFIN: So are you. Because the individual finally has to make his own decision or he's not a human being.

MR. CARY: But you're making judgments for others.

MR. LEIBMAN: What if Reverend Coffin can make superior judgments to yours? Isn't that what he is saying?

MR. CARY: You're saying, Dr. Coffin, that these things are right, that they're good.

DR. COFFIN: In my opinion they are and who else's opinion have I got? Who is to make these decisions?

MR. CARY: I think society is a better judge, as a matter of fact.

DR. COFFIN: In other words, you're just going to cop out on your own individual conscience?

MR. CARY: No, I don't cop out on these things. I just don't think anybody's that omniscient.

DR. COFFIN: I agree with you. All our vision is partial and it's flawed not only by our finiteness but by our sinfulness. But I refuse to say that any human being has a right to give up his conscience to somebody else, to some organization. Truth is our authority, not some authority our truth.

MR. CARY: That's why it's the truth.

DR. COFFIN: And we have to make these decisions. Nobody else can make them for us. It's a great dilemma. It may seem very prideful, it may seem egotistical and very often it gets very self-righteous, there's no question about it.

MR. CARY: Yes, and what seems to be the truth today may be something else tomorrow.

DR. COFFIN: But the other alternative is all persons simply saying, "Well, let somebody else decide for me, I'm just going to chicken out." And that's the mass mentality, isn't it?

MR. CARY: No.

DR. COFFIN: What is the difference then?

MR. CARY: I'm asking questions, not answering them.

DR. COFFIN: All right, I don't see how anybody but the individual can decide for that individual as to whether this war is just or unjust. Who else is going to make that decision? The government? That's the way they do it in the Soviet Union.

MR. CARY: Don't you feel a little humble about making judgments about this?

DR. COFFIN: Yes, I sure do.

MR. CARY: That's good.

DR. COFFIN: But, might I say I'd rather be a little prideful than to be totally cowardly.

DANIEL MOSKOWITZ, McGraw-Hill: I'm just wondering whether you, Mr. Leibman, disagree with what's just been said? You said something earlier about the difference between imitative heroes and real heroes. Were you suggesting that real heroes have rights that imitative heroes don't have? Then, of course, the question is: How do you tell the difference between the two?

MR. LEIBMAN: The point I was trying to make was that in the long agony of looking for some system of justice we had to have some real heroes—those real heroes, by definition, would have said, "Ah, what you've got in the Constitution and what you're doing with it, that's what we dreamt about, that was our great dream."

Now we've got a real job to do with this system with its levers. We no longer have to be civil disobedients. A few minutes ago the Reverend Coffin said, "Maybe what we're talking about is that the means are ends and the beginning of the search." The creation of the American system said to the people, in effect: you have no right to be disobedient anymore. That's precisely my position. We've drawn some foul lines and we've given you an apparatus for change that solves the dilemma of your consciences and of all the clashing and conflicts of justices and interests. From time to time the rules have to change. This is why we have an apparatus that is constantly working on the means. It assumes different moralities, different consciences, different hopes for justice and it's given us a mechanism for reconciling them. What's unique about this mechanism is that it can be weighed, balanced, and evaluated regularly.

MR. MOSKOWITZ: The time for heroes has passed?

MR. LEIBMAN: That's right. The time for another kind of hero—those with effort, with sweat, with perspiration, and not with headlines—has now come because our problems have increased in complexity. I've said it this way to myself sometimes. When one man lives on a thousand acres of ground, we don't care whether he shoots a cannon at midnight or uses the stream for a toilet facility. But when we compress a thousand men into one acre, we are infringing on so many liberties and inviting so many clashes that we must constantly work at handling that complexity. As the complexities increase, it is even more necessary for great heroes to go to work on new frontiers of human nature and human conflict. Thank God, our system provides the apparatus, the research laboratory, that permits honest research, honest testing and development.

A simple example is what happens when it's decided we must have public housing, and so we rush into building it. Are multi-storied buildings the answer? Their sameness— does that do something to human psychology, et cetera? We must keep re-evaluating these things, recognizing man's nature. You see what we've left out here is our animal nature and our rational nature, our savage nature and the divine spark in our nature, or however you want to put it.

Every time there are two of us, there are conflicts and the more we have of sardine society, the more difficult are our problems. My God, let's rededicate heroes to using this wonderful research laboratory that has never existed anywhere else.

MR. BERNSTEIN: This is going to be a rather simplistic example but I want to ask Dr. Coffin how he would handle two moral questions arising out of the following situation: I, as an individual, know that Joe Doakes is an evil creature.

73

I know that he has committed terrible crimes, the most heinous type of crimes one can imagine. I know this. It's not imagination. And he's escaped the legal consequences for one technical reason or another. And after he's been acquitted—let's say on these technical grounds—he boasts that he committed the crimes. My conscience tells me that this man ought to die.

Now my first question is: although the law forbids murder, am I justified morally in killing him? Second, am I justified in asking someone else to join me in killing him—or persuading someone else who might be more effective to do it? Or, should the rule of law, decency and civilization limit me to trying to persuade everybody I know, perhaps even organizing a movement to get the law amended so that men like Joe Doakes cannot escape the just consequences of their crimes?

What rights do my conscience give me in that situation? I have taken an easy case because everybody abhores cold-blooded, deliberate murder where it isn't a tyrant or a despot that's involved. What's the answer?

DR. COFFIN: I think you gave it, didn't you?

MR. BERNSTEIN: No, I want your answer. I know what mine is. How would you decide this?

Clearly, I take it, you agree that the most that I am permitted to do morally is to try to persuade as many people as I can, that we must use the procedures which are available—and we'll assume they are available ultimately—to change the law so that my goal can be accomplished through valid, constitutional, legal means.

DR. COFFIN: My problem is with your goal. If your goal is a satisfying one to you—but I don't think it satisfies your more generous nature. It sounds to me as if you're out for your pound of flesh and as Freud said—

MR. BERNSTEIN: No. You have to accept my premise.

DR. COFFIN: The demands of justice are but a modification of envy.

MR. BERNSTEIN: No, wait a minute. You have to accept the premise of my example.

DR. COFFIN: Look, if you have a sick conscience—it's perfectly reasonable to expect that some people have very sick consciences.

MR. BERNSTEIN: What do you mean by sick? Do you mean that it's not a right conscience, that there's something—

DR. COFFIN: It's not particularly loving.

MR. BERNSTEIN: You don't know what I want to change the law to. I want him to be punished, but that doesn't necessarily mean I approve of capital punishment.

DR. COFFIN: Maybe you ought to be rehabilitated.

MR. BERNSTEIN: I want him to be confined so he doesn't do the same thing again sometime. There's nothing sick about that.

DR. COFFIN: It's pretty unbiblical. Where's the mercy? There's no mercy in what you're talking about, and therefore, it's unjust. You're not interested in the guy's rehabilitation. You want his death.

MR. BERNSTEIN: I didn't say I wanted his death.

DR. COFFIN: I thought you did.

MR. BERNSTEIN: I want him to be punished in a way so that he can't do any harm anymore. I don't have to be an advocate of capital punishment to want him isolated.

DR. COFFIN: Now, look, if you didn't say you wanted his death, there's no simple formula I can give you. I'm trying to show the complexity of this issue—it's not simple at all. I haven't succeeded perhaps.

MR. BERNSTEIN: No, I think you're picking and choosing your cases.

DR. COFFIN: There's no easy answer. I think you can put it in a paradoxical form. You can say every man has the obligation to obey the law and every man upon occasion has the duty to disobey it.

MR. BERNSTEIN: Does he have the right to persuade others to disobey it? This is what I'm asking you.

DR. COFFIN: You know, I think Martin Luther King was right in Birmingham to say "You should not be segregated."

MR. BERNSTEIN: I am willing to concede this example for the simple reason that I think slavery was wrong from the beginning—and particularly given what our Constitution says.

DR. COFFIN: How about the labor movement when people said to others, "I think we have to engage in a boycott, boys; the managers ain't going to get the message until we do"?

MR. BERNSTEIN: I think if the law prohibits boycott, and it does now—

DR. COFFIN: And it did then.

MR. BERNSTEIN: —I think they have an obligation to obey the law and then try to get it changed. The labor movement has been trying to do that for many years.

DR. COFFIN: Yes, but you know how things are changed.

MR. BERNSTEIN: And they haven't succeeded.

DR. COFFIN: How did the French get through a 40-hour week and vacation with pay and all the rest of it in the 1930s? They succeeded because when Leon Blum was in the government they had a reasonable man who was basically on their side in power. Then they had an absolutely massive wave of strikes, and the result was a combination of their action and the reasonable man in government who could make a positive response to it. Without either Leon Blum or the strikes the French workers would not have had the same success.

MR. BERNSTEIN: You happen to approve of those ends and so do I, but—

DR. COFFIN: I'm asking if they would have succeeded.

MR. BERNSTEIN: I'll answer that by simply saying that if they had waited 10 years and tried to change the law in France, they might have gotten the same result. And by not waiting, something was risked. Now supposing the objective was different—for example to take over the factories?

DR. COFFIN: That's what I say, the end justifies the means.

MR. BERNSTEIN: Where do you draw the line?

DR. COFFIN: That's the problem. I don't say that the end justifies *all* means. I'm trying not to draw any lines because I can't draw any lines. You're trying to get some

77

nice clean formula and principle. I'm saying human beings cannot be subjected to that.

MR. BERNSTEIN: I'd like a list or a catalogue—

DR. COFFIN: Pigeon holes are for pigeons.

MR. BERNSTEIN: —I'd like a catalogue of the instances in which you think deliberate disobedience of the law, of a constitutional law, a valid law—not one which is not being tested, because there's a procedure for that—

DR. COFFIN: I gave you my answer for that. At the very opening I gave you a whole slew of instances in which I thought disobedience was justified.

JOHN STEEVES, Center for Strategic and International Studies, formerly United States ambassador: I'd like to get back into an area that I think is more important than at least parts of this recent exchange. I think a good share of your argument, Reverend Coffin, is based upon the premise that this nation of which we are a part is basically evil; therefore, any means is justifiable that brings about partial or total revolution in order to change it. I question that premise. I don't think that the United States is perfect but I do think that its institutions and its methods for bringing about justice and its democratic means of settling problems come as close to perfection as those of any society that has ever been pulled together.

DR. COFFIN: If you were a ghetto Black, would you believe that?

MR. STEEVES: Let me go on. Some of your parallels from history are pretty far awry. You talked about Jesus coming into the world and kicking over the traces against the regime and you assumed that it was pretty good. Remember that was the period of Herod and remember what happened to the children about the time that Christ was born. It wasn't so pure. I don't think there is a sound parallel between Herod of the Roman Empire and the United States, and I resent any suggestion of one.

Another thing: I might go along with you about people demonstrating or people using extra-legal means in their protests and all the rest of it, if they were pure-minded about it and if they had constructive goals in mind. But the trouble is that when you talk to that rabble or hear what they say in their conventions or read what they print, you find it's not towards constructive goals at all.

Now the democratic way is to elect authorities to decide on a collective basis what is probably the best course for this nation to take. Ours is one of the only countries in the world that does it, and I think this is the safest way.

If an individual gets down to the matter of private conscience, this is one of the only countries under God's heaven that gives a person the right to decide what he will do with his own conscience. For example, a conscientious objector does not need to go to war; he can do other service. He can write and say what he pleases. But he does not have the right to go out and interfere with the rights of other people, which is what you are trying to justify in order to support a revolution against those things in the United States government that you don't happen to like.

Now there's where you're really off your base altogether.

DR. COFFIN: Why are you so scared.

MR. STEEVES: Because I happen to have lived 40 years overseas and have seen what happens in countries where these kinds of emotions run rampant and what happens finally to curb them. This country is one of the last bastions on the earth where constitutional law still abides, where there still is democratic government and justice and where people still have access to see their own rights fulfilled. Fellows that support what you support are going to keep this type of thing up until those rights are overthrown. That's what I'm scared of.

DR. COFFIN: Have you seen any country that was truly democratic and where there was a high degree of justice overthrown by rabble?

MR. BERNSTEIN: Social democratic Germany.

MR. STEEVES: Yes, sure.

DR. COFFIN: I don't think that was a beautiful example of justice there, was it?

MR. LEIBMAN: Pre-Hitler Czechoslovakia.

DR. COFFIN: Aha, Czechoslovakia, you mean the Soviet interference there.

MR. LEIBMAN: Before Hitler, before the Soviet intervention.

DR. COFFIN: All right, I agree. But what I'm trying to say is why I think you're so scared. There's a very small group in this country that are like a parasite in the sense that they can only feed on disease in the body politic. Now if the body politic is healthy, you don't get this type of commotion. You say this country is the finest in the world. I ask you, sir, if you were a poor Black in Harlem, would you be talking that way?

MR. STEEVES: I don't know if I would.

DR. COFFIN: If you did, you would show remarkable insensitivity to the fate of your fellow man.

MR. STEEVES: Let me quote a Black attorney that I happened to have heard with my own ears. Judge Sampson, who comes from the city of Chicago—

DR. COFFIN: I'm not talking about judges.

MR. STEEVES: She's a Black—

DR. COFFIN: I'm talking about guys who have not had that much of a chance, in housing—

MR. STEEVES: —and she's pretty militant at times.

DR. COFFIN: —schooling, medicine or any other thing.

MR. STEEVES: But when she was being baited on this business overseas, I heard her say to a crowd of Indians: "You show me a colored country that has made as much progress for their colored people in 800 years as we have made in the United States and I'll listen to your arguments."

MR. LEIBMAN: I think I'd like to make three points.

First, it's unfair, Bill, to use the word scared. I think what Mr. Steeves said reflects a sensitivity to how fragile the idea of an open society is and how particularly fragile it is with technological change, economic problems and all those many human problems that go with our being the world's greatest conglomerate. Nobody's ever tried to balance so many elements. We are worried about the fragile nature of this delicate laboratory and we're terribly worried about losing it.

My second point is that when we try to do something or create something between the illegal and the legal in this mechanism, we're trying to do the impossible. There ain't no in between. The apparatus must be preserved because it is capable of constantly redrawing its foul lines, and nothing you ever do will create anything better than that.

My third point has to do with what you keep repeating about the ghetto Black. I hate to have anybody who opposes civil disobedience be put in the category of a fascist or a racist or an inhumane person. Let me refer the Black analogy to the example of Israel. Here is a country of only 3 million people that is welcoming back its Jews with long and varied historical heritages. With its African Jews, black Jews, and so forth, Israel has the same terrible cultural gaps, ethical gaps, value gaps, and the same terrible dilemma we have here. I hope we know that these survivors of Auschwitz and Dachau have compassion, but the problem of bridging these 800 year gaps, or even 100 years, is a desperate one.

Now, as to our ghetto Blacks. I worked long hours with Whitney Young. In my last discussion with him, we were planning to implement a plan with the support of certain Black leaders in this country that was based on the notion that maybe we have been grabbing the wrong end of the stick. Maybe these mass approaches can't work. We would start with local organizations in some test areas to see how we could get a good relationship between a neighborhood and its fire department.

Because, you see, one of the problems we have had is that there are a number of success stories in the Black ghetto—which may encompass a two-block community, a six-block community, or an eight-block community—where things begin to work; but then the gangs from across the street try to take part of that action. We felt that we had to start further back with the laborious job of education through reason with compassion and say, "Here is why the fire department's good for you. Here's why your hospital ought to be saved. Here's why the schools need support."

But our chief conclusion was that massive programs do not get to the heart of the problem. You have to take people as people and really personally educate them in small groups to these new areas.

MR. MILLER: Yes, I keep hearing what are not even thinly veiled attacks on Dr. Coffin and keep hearing it said that the type of civil disobedience he espouses will inevitably lead to the kind of violence that will overthrow the apparatus. I'm sorry you used the word, apparatus, Mr. Leibman, because I don't think it's a particularly good word to describe the non-system we have in this country.

I happen to think that a far greater threat to this country than the civil disobedience that he advocates and that the youngsters performed on May Day is the injustice of the system, the obvious injustice that we all know exists, that is documented every day by administration after administration, by study after study. To sit here and tell us that some young people and some men of the cloth who are committing some acts of civil disobedience are going to lead to the overthrow of this apparatus absolutely astounds me.

What's going to lead to the overthrow of the system, if anything does, is the continual injustice it keeps perpetrating on a great many Americans.

MR. LEIBMAN: May I ask you something? I don't understand your dichotomy. Do you accept that this is a good apparatus, a good system, as a system?

MR. MILLER: I called it a non-system, Mr. Leibman.

MR. LEIBMAN: Then you don't recognize as a system the Constitution, separation of powers, representative government, et cetera? You don't consider these things a system?

MR. MILLER: I accept the abstractions of the Constitution as valid. I don't accept the reality of the injustice as it is working and has been working, and for you to sit up there and keep saying that this system or non-system or apparatus is going to correct these injustices and that we've got to discourse reasonably and we've got to go on accepting it without any more than that—is really quite astounding to me.

MR. LEIBMAN: I can't accept what you're saying. Do you have a different system or do you have a different non-system?

You see, we can all make speeches about injustice. But when you start telling me about justice, I require that you tell me how to get there.

MR. MILLER: When the system or non-system does not provide justice it will lead to excesses and I think some of the excesses we are seeing did not come from Dr. Coffin preaching civil disobedience. I don't attribute to him that great power and I don't think he accepts it.

MR. LEIBMAN: What I want to know is how, in your system or non-system, are we going to handle all these injustices. I think that an emotional appeal about system and non-system avoids the issue.

MR. MILLER: You're the one that's been making an emotional appeal.

MR. LEIBMAN: Have you got a system?

MR. MILLER: You've been saying we must uphold the apparatus at any cost. That's emotional appeal.

84

MR. LEIBMAN: No, I'm saying here is a real system that's done better than anything else anybody has ever thought of, ever, in any place.

MR. MILLER: We discriminate more. Our medical system is not all that good.

MR. LEIBMAN: But is there some other system—

DR. COFFIN: The Soviets do better in medicine.

MR. LEIBMAN: Then you prefer that system over this system?

DR. COFFIN: No, I didn't say I preferred the Soviet system. I said when I'm sick I don't mind having a doctor around, and I think it's a pretty bad thing when the hospital emergency room has to be the family physician for millions of folk in this country, given the great resources of our great, wonderful nation. I'm not saying civil disobedience is the only thing that's going to work. But it's one of many things that may be necessary if we're going to try to get people to wake up to the fact—

MR. LEIBMAN: And I'm saying that you're not going to wake them up with excesses. You're going to polarize them.

DR. COFFIN: You have to recognize also, Morris, what Martin Luther King meant when he said that the United States Congress is the greatest purveyor of violence in this world; he was talking about indifference.

Now [to Mr. Steeves] I'll speak to your Pontius Pilate situation in Rome, sir. Pilate was the important one, not Herod. Let's just take this question of violence. If your heart can go out to St. Peter lopping off the ear of the high priest's servant in the Garden of Gethsemane because he was so moved by the injustices about to be perpetrated through his laws, then, by God, your heart ought to be able to go out to anybody who takes to violence or takes to arms because of the sufferings of others.

MR. LEIBMAN: He also rejected Christ three times before the cock crowed.

DR. COFFIN: That is not germane to this point. [Laughter.] The point is that violence can be an expression of charity whereas indifference can only be the perfection of egoism. And I ask you if it's worse to have blood on your hands or water like Pilate? Now King was quite clear that in having water on your hands like Pilate—

MR. MacQUEENEY: Christ rejected that: "Put up your swords; if I have legions I can call upon them."

DR. COFFIN: Right but not to Peter he didn't. He did not say that.

FATHER JOSEPH BECKER, Jesuit Center for Social Studies: I'd like to make an attempt at focusing a little more sharply what I suspect is the real issue here. I may be wrong but I have an idea you'll agree with me.

Violation of the law as a form of force, of course, is subject to the usual ethical rules for the use of force. They've been worked out in great detail with regard to war, which is the final form of force: that your objective must be sufficiently important, that force is the only way to achieve it, that the means have to be commensurate to a reasonable likelihood of success and so forth. There really isn't any difference, I don't think, between the two speakers here on the fundamental ethics involved.

There are times when force is all right. There are times when it isn't. To really get a joining of the issues one could do one of two things.

One could take up instance after instance and say, "How do these principles apply here?" There'd be no end to that.

Or there is another way and a number of us have touched on this. There is the feeling that, if one starts to use force too easily, it gains a momentum that you cannot stop and in the long run results in greater losses than gains. In economics, my own field, we usually say that probably the most important distinction to make in economics is between short-run effects and long-run effects.

I myself am inclined temperamentally to be in sympathy with the sort of thing that Dr. Coffin is doing and that the gentleman across the way has been espousing. At the same time, I have become aware of what seems to me to be a momentum which is being generated and that gives me pause. I could give seven or eight indices of this momentum but let me take just two that might be of some interest.

One is in modern art. I've always felt that art gives you in its purest form what is taking place in a culture. It seems to me that in modern art we find a growing relativist individualism, a shaking off of all kinds of restraints. The individual simply says, "This is what I feel, this is what I want to do. I do my thing, you do your thing and that's it."

Second, what's happening within the Jesuit order and other religious orders? Being a member of the Jesuit order, I have a firsthand experience of this. Our whole pattern of life is changing and what is interesting about it is the process by which it is changing. It's not changing by having meetings, discussing questions, deciding what to do. It's being changed by people voting with their feet, by just doing different things. And this is within a group of people who have taken a vow of obedience.

Things of this sort—what's happening in modern art, what's happening within a religious order—make me ask myself whether there isn't something rather profound, something rather at the core of things, taking place.

I'm inclined to dismiss it. I don't think it's quite that important, but I'm not sure. It may be that the growth of the communications media, this ease with which an idea moves, and the rising level of education may place more people in opposition to the institution all the time. It may be that we're setting loose forces which can disrupt our whole society.

All I'm saying at the moment is that I suspect the real issue is that some of us see a danger and some don't and that this is what really separates us because it's a long-run effect and there's no way of being sure about it.

MODERATOR GORALSKI: May I ask you now, Dr. Coffin and Mr. Leibman, for a brief concluding statement.

DR. COFFIN: I would pick up where Father Becker left off. I think that there's another difference if you turn what he said around. Some are afraid that the forces of dissolution are being loosed. Others are afraid that the individual has already been dissolved, has been dehumanized and a society that is more interested in institutional growth than individual growth, more interested in efficiency than in the humanity of human beings, that the individual has been sacrificed to institutions and systems so that in fact the problem is not the dissolution of individuals but the reconstruction of individuals who already have been to a large degree dissolved.

Now, take the war protestors who went to Canada, and this I'm sure would offend many of us in this room. But yet they made an individual choice, they behaved as human beings. I'm not saying that all their motives were pure but that they behaved as human beings because they took responsibility for themselves and their own decisions and made a decision. In contrast, the general pattern in this country has been to let other people make decisions, or institutions or the government, and we have lost some sense of our own individual humanity.

So I think one can almost judge these various actions and changes in terms of one question: to what degree are we humanizing human beings? Have we really looked at our system carefully enough to discover how humane or inhumane it may be?

I think the real differences in this room are mainly in the analysis of how important it is to be highly critical of our society for the sake of our truly patriotic desire to make this country more fully reflect the best in human beings. Some of us have been very deeply concerned that America has not represented the best in terms of justice and peace and mercy. Most of these protestors have been basically for an effort to recapture some of the humanity which has been lost.

Now I don't say for a moment that there aren't a great many perversions, but you, as a good Jesuit, Father, will know, misuse does not contradict proper use. We have to be very careful that we don't allow misuse of things to distract our attention from the proper use of things.

MR. LEIBMAN: The many incidents recounted merely serve to point out that man can be human and he can be inhuman. He is a creature of jealousy and laziness, of envy, of cruelty, of indifference, and our problem is to reconcile his good and his evil nature.

I suggest it's only through a system. Non-system means power and power is certainly no way to get justice. Therefore, I would suggest that every human being, as a human, not as a god, owes an obligation to the highest morality, which is to seek the system that handles the most injustices with justice —that understands that its success will bring new problems and that continuing flexibility is required to meet the needs of man's nature and man's inhumanity to man.

I would suggest that we really shouldn't be talking about new forms of disobedience but how to better appeal to man's reason and how to handle more complex questions. How do we use petition, assembly, free speech, and persuasion for developing better answers, better alternatives? Maybe those of us who are for this continuing breakthrough aren't scared, aren't frightened. But we recognize we're paying the price of our successes and I say to those who want to take the next move, "Make sure that you don't throw away the successes and make sure that you understand that the very success of our system means more complexity and more difficulty as more people participate." The complex society our success has produced, with its greater problems, demands a higher civility. We need more civility, not disobedience.

NOTES TO
SECOND LECTURE

NOTES

[1] John Courtney Murray, S.J., "America's Four Conspiracies," *Religion in America,* ed. John Cogley (New York: Meridian Books, Inc., 1962), pp. 16-17.

[2] George F. Kennan, *Democracy and the Student Left* (New York: Bantam Books, 1968), p. 16.

[3] "The Speech of Justice," *The Spirit of Liberty,* ed. Irving Dilliard (New York: Vintage Books, 1959), p. 12.

[4] Henry David Thoreau, *Walden and On the Duty of Civil Disobedience* (New York: The New American Library, 1960), p. 222.

[5] Charles E. Whittaker and William Sloane Coffin, Jr., *Law, Order and Civil Disobedience* (Washington, D. C.: American Enterprise Institute, 1967), p. 39.

[6] 85 *Harvard Law Review* 898 (1972).

[7] Alexander M. Bickel, "The Revolution of Unreason," *The New Republic,* October 17, 1970, p. 21.

[8] Ibid.

[9] Whittaker and Coffin, *Civil Disobedience,* p. 47.

[10] Dr. David A. Hamburg, "An Evolutionary Perspective on Human Aggressiveness," in *Modern Psychiatry and Clinical Research,* ed. Daniel Offer & Daniel X. Freedman (New York: Basic Books, Inc., 1972), pp. 40-41.

[11] Dr. Alfred A. Messer, " 'Self-defense' Can Kill You," *Chicago Sun Times,* Sunday, February 20, 1972, p. 33.

[12] Murray, "America's Four Conspiracies," p. 24.

[13] Ibid., p. 23.